A Soldier's Creed

I am an American Soldier.

I am a warrior and a member of a team.

I serve the people of the United States and live the Army Values.

I will always place the mission first.

I will never accept defeat.

I will never quit.

I will never leave a fallen comrade.

I am disciplined, physically and mentally
tough, trained and proficient in my warrior tasks and drills.

I always maintain my arms, my equipment,
and myself.

I am an expert and I am a professional.

I stand ready to deploy, engage, and destroy
the enemies of the United States of America in close combat.

I am a guardian of freedom and the American way of life.

I am an American Soldier.

Other books in the **When I Grow Up I Want To Be...**
children's book series by Wigu Publishing:

When I Grow Up I Want To Be...a Teacher!

When I Grow Up I Want To Be...a Firefighter!

When I Grow Up I Want To Be...in the U.S. Navy!

When I Grow Up I Want To Be...a Veterinarian!

When I Grow Up I Want To Be...a Nurse!

Look for these titles in the **When I Grow Up I Want To Be...**
children's book series soon:

When I Grow Up I Want To Be...a Good Person!

When I Grow Up I Want To Be...a World Traveler!

When I Grow Up I Want To Be...a Race Car Driver!

When I Grow Up I Want To Be...a Police Officer!

When I Grow Up I Want To Be... Green!

When I Grow Up I Want To Be...a Rock Star!

W**When I Grow Up I Want To Be...**in the U.S. Air Force!

Cuando Crezca Quiero Ser... coming soon!

Please visit www.whenigrowupbooks.com for more information.
Please like us at www.facebook.com/whenigrowupbooksbywigu.

When I Grow Up I Want To Be...®

in the U.S. Army!

Jake Learns about
the U.S. Army.

Wigu Publishing | Sun Valley, ID

Copyright © 2014 by Wigu Publishing, LLC

Illustrations copyright © 2014 by Wigu Publishing, LLC

All rights reserved. No part of this publication may be reproduced, distributed, or transmitted in any form or by any means, including photocopying, recording, or other electronic or mechanical methods, without the prior written permission of the publisher, except in the case of brief quotations embodied in critical reviews and certain other noncommercial uses permitted by copyright law. For permission requests, please write to the publisher at the address below.

Library of Congress Control Number: 2014906391

ISBN 978-1-939973-06-1

When I Grow Up I Want To Be... is a registered trademark of Wigu Publishing, LLC. The word Wigu and the Wigu logo are registered trademarks of Wigu Publishing, LLC. The words When I Grow Up... and Cuando Crezca Quiero Ser... are trademarks and/or registered trademarks of Wigu Publishing, LLC.

Wigu Publishing is a collaboration among talented and creative individuals working together to publish informative and fun books for our children. Our titles serve to introduce children to the people in their communities who serve others through their vocations. Wigu's books are unique in that they help our children to visualize the abundant opportunities that exist for them to be successful and to make a difference. Our goal is to inspire the great leaders and thinkers of tomorrow.

Second edition, paperback, 2014

10 9 8 7 6 5 4 3 2 1

Quantity sales: Special discounts are available on quantity purchases by corporations, associations, promotional organizations, and others. For details, please contact the publisher at

Wigu Publishing

P.O. Box 1800

Sun Valley, ID 83353

inquiries@wigupublishing.com

Please visit our website at www.whenigrowupbooks.com for more information.

Proudly printed and bound in the United States of America.

The publisher gratefully acknowledges the assistance of the
United States Department of Defense and the U.S. Army,
without whose help this book would not be possible.

We would also like to thank active and retired members of the
Army community for providing invaluable guidance and assistance
in the creation of this book.

Please support our Wounded Warriors.
Visit www.woundedwarriorproject.org for information
on how you can help our heroes.

For more information on the U.S. Army, please visit www.goarmy.com.

This is the story of a boy named Jake. Jake has a school project: "What do you want to be when you grow up?" Jake picks a soldier in the U.S. Army. Here is how he learned all about it.

Jake's teacher, Miss Brooks, stood in front of the whole class and said, "I have a question for each of you, one you might want to ask yourself. What do you want to be when you grow up?"

Almost all the kids in the class raised their hands at once.

Not Jake.

Dakota raised her hand and said, "I want to be a rock star!"

Tommy shot his hand up and said, "I want to be a U.S. Navy SEAL!"

Jake couldn't think of an answer because he wanted to be so many things.

Miss Brooks held up her hand to stop the class. "Don't tell me yet, please. Here is what we are going to do. You will each tell me with our next class project. You may write about your choice of careers. You may make a poster. You may even dress up as what you want to be or bring something about your choice to class and tell us about it."

Jake's brain was in a jumble. There were a ton of things he wanted to be when he grew up: a race car driver, the president, a firefighter, a scientist, a secret agent, a soldier, a veterinarian, or maybe even a rock star!

This is almost like dressing up for Halloween, thought Jake. *But without the candy.*

Jake looked over at his friend Hannah. Her hand wasn't raised either. "Don't you know what you want to be?"

Hannah smiled and said, "Of course I know, but I'm not telling anyone yet."

Jake thought, *Why does everyone know but me?*

The bell rang. It was time to go home. Jake thought, *I bet Hannah doesn't really know. She's just pretending.*

Jake got on the school bus and headed home. He thought of all the things he wanted to be when he grew up.

When Jake's dad got home from work, Jake told him about the class project. "I don't know which one to pick," said Jake.

"Just pick one you like," said Dad.

That doesn't help me much, Jake thought. *I like them all.*

As if Dad could read Jake's mind, he suggested, "Let's narrow it down, ok? How about a firefighter? Or a police officer? How about a soldier? I was in the Army, you know."

Jake knew. He had heard all about it many times.

"Maybe a soldier would work," said Jake. "I might want to be a soldier."

"Well," said Dad, smiling, "you don't have to join the Army tomorrow."

"I know," said Jake. "I did a poster for my last project. Maybe for this project, I could dress up like an Army soldier and talk about it. But I need a really cool uniform."

"I have an idea," said Dad. "Tomorrow is Saturday, so why don't we go down to the Army surplus store? They have all kinds of Army supplies, uniforms, badges, and medals. We can find something for you there."

"Awesome!" said Jake.

The next day, Jake and Dad drove across town to a store with a sign that read: "GI Surplus."

"We're here," said Dad, as they pulled up to the curb.

"Dad, look at all the Army stuff in the window!" exclaimed Jake. "This is so great. I didn't even know there were stores like this. I'll bet I'm the only one in my school who does!"

Dad said, "Do you know what GI stands for?"

"Gee, I want a bigger allowance?" answered Jake.

"Nice try," Dad chuckled. "GI means 'Government Issue.'"

Too bad, Jake thought. *I wonder if I can get a bigger allowance anyway!*

The letters **"GI"** stand for Government Issue. U.S. Army soldiers are called GIs because everything they wear and carry is issued, or given to them, by the U.S. government.

U.S. Army GI equipped and ready for action

As Jake and Dad walked into the store, Jake pointed to a display mannequin. "He's dressed up like George Washington!"

"That's because he's wearing the uniform worn by Washington's soldiers in the Continental Army," said Dad.

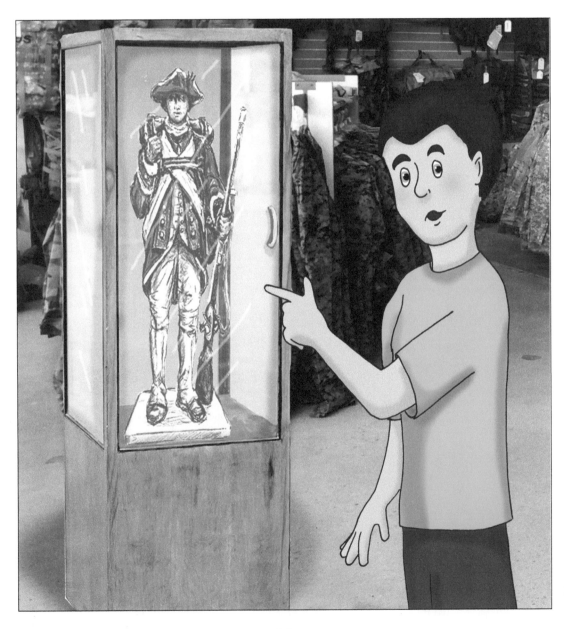

The United States Army traces its history back to 1775 and the formation of the Continental Army. Led by General George Washington, these early patriots helped win our independence from Great Britain in the American Revolutionary War. Without these brave men, there would be no United States. Today's soldier is the same kind of patriot and just as important to our nation.

"There is nothing so likely to produce peace as to be well prepared to meet the enemy."
—George Washington
Commander of the Continental Army
First President of the United States

"I'm going to need an Army uniform, like a jacket and some pants," said Jake. "What about these?"

"Good place to start," said Dad. "That's a Class A uniform."

Jake grinned. "Maybe it will help me get an 'A' on my project!"

"Maybe," said Dad.

"Look at all those badges and pins!" said Jake.

"Those show rank," replied Dad. "Rank shows the soldiers who is boss of whom."

"They would look awesome on my uniform! Can I get some, please?"

"That's what we're here for," said Dad.

"How many can I have?" asked Jake. "Which ones should I get?"

Dad smiled. "Those pins with bars, leaves, and eagles are for the officers. The stars are for the generals. I was a Sergeant, so I had three stripes."

Jake knew that Dad had been a Sergeant in the Army. He had heard all about Dad's Army adventures. Sometimes when Dad told a story, he'd bring out his old Army pictures and Sergeant's arm patch.

Jake liked hearing Dad's stories over and over because they were never quite the same.

Four-Star General Norman Schwarzkopf

Each and every soldier is critical to the Army's ability to defend our country, our freedoms, and our way of life.

The U.S. Army has both enlisted soldiers and commissioned officers.

Enlisted soldiers are known for their sense of duty and the sacrifices they make for our country. Enlisted soldiers are trained for a lot of different jobs depending on their skills and the Army's needs. An enlisted soldier's rank ranges from Private to Sergeant Major of the Army.

Commissioned officers are the managers and planners of the Army. They lead the enlisted soldiers. To be a commissioned officer, you must be a college graduate. Officers' ranks range from Second Lieutenant to General of the Army.

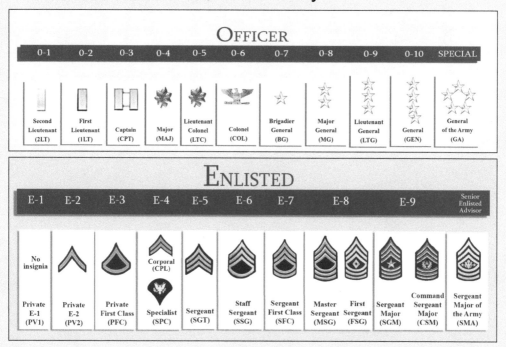

Jake said, "There are a ton of different patches for sale. Can I pick out a few for my project? How many can I have?"

"Patches show the soldier's unit," Dad said. "Let's pick one."

"How about two?" asked Jake.

"One is enough," said Dad.

The Army is not made up of just combat, or fighting, soldiers. There are a lot of jobs to be done. For example, you can be a helicopter pilot, a computer operator, or a tank driver. There are Army doctors, teachers, nurses, mechanics, dentists, lawyers—even Military Police and firefighters.

No matter what the job or rank, each soldier's duty is to protect our country, our friends, and our allies.

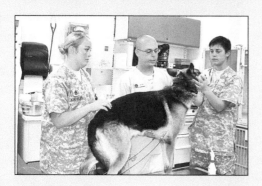

Jake picked up a patch that showed two crossed swords. "How about this one?"

Dad studied the patch. "That is an Infantry Brigade arm patch. They are the foot soldiers."

"I like the swords. Why are some patches brown and others have a lot of colors?" asked Jake.

"The darker ones were made for combat. They blend in better with the uniform—like camouflage. They don't stick out."

The Infantry is made up of foot soldiers. Foot soldiers march, hike, and fight on the ground. They are the backbone of the Army.

"This is cool," said Jake, picking up a new patch.

"That one is for the Airborne division," said Dad. "They are Infantry soldiers who are brought in by plane or helicopter to where they are needed."

"I thought that the Infantry was just foot soldiers," said Jake.

"They are foot soldiers as soon as they hit the ground," said Dad.

Airborne troops are important in battle because they can surprise, shock, and overwhelm an enemy. In humanitarian missions, they can bring help quickly.

Airborne troops reach their missions in several ways. They can parachute down from flying planes, be dropped in by hovering helicopters, or be unloaded off of an aircraft that has landed.

Jake saw another patch he liked. "What is this one for?"

"That's for the soldiers of the Field Artillery," said Dad. "They handle the cannons, missiles, and rockets."

Artillery refers to the Army's large, heavy weapons. At the beginning of a battle, the Army might bombard an enemy with artillery. The artillery fire helps to weaken the enemy before the Infantry is sent in.

One of the first pieces of artillery was the catapult. Catapults were like giant slingshots that hurled rocks and fireballs at the enemy on the battlefield or over high castle walls. Catapults also launched all kinds of annoying and disgusting things like dead animals and even poop!

Today the U.S. Army defends our country with new powerful, high-tech artillery, from heavy cannons to long-range rockets.

"Alright!" said Jake. "I want one of the Artillery patches for sure. Maybe two?"

"One is fine. You can't be in two units at the same time."

Jake thought, *What does that matter? I'm just a kid!*

"Or would you like a patch like this one? It's for the Armored Brigade. They are the tank soldiers," said Dad.

The modern tank's cannon fires deadly explosive shells to destroy faraway targets or blow holes in enemy walls close by. On top of the tank sits the machine gun that protects the tank soldiers inside.

U.S. ARMY M1A2 ABRAMS TANK

1. Commander's machine gun
2. Machine gun ammunition
3. Hatch
4. Turret ring
5. Hull
6. Turret
7. Engine air intake
8. Engine compartment
9. Drive sprocket
10. Link
11. Road wheel
12. Side armor
13. Track
14. Driver's hatch
15. Driver's optics
16. Main gun
17. Fume extractor
18. Periscope

Named after General Creighton Abrams

"What's this horse patch?"

"Air Cavalry," said Dad. "They are the helicopter soldiers."

Jake was puzzled. "Why horses?"

"That's because the first cavalry used horses."

The word "cavalry" refers to horses. Originally the U.S. Cavalry charged into battles on horseback just like cavalries all over the world have done for centuries. Some countries even used camels and elephants. Today, the U.S. Cavalry is called Air Cavalry, or Air Cav, because the soldiers fly in aircraft instead of riding horses. The horse on the patch honors their history. The Air Cavalry is one of the most decorated units of the Army.

There are still horses in the Army, but they are mostly for parades and ceremonies.

"What about those ribbons?" asked Jake.

"Those are service ribbons and medals. They are given for every action, tour of duty, and war service and for acts of great bravery," said Dad.

While serving our nation, soldiers can be sent to almost anywhere in the world—from Middle Eastern deserts to deep jungles and frozen tundra. Soldiers may be away from friends, home, and family for a long time. Soldiers sacrifice much to serve their country, sometimes even their lives.

For their **dedication and valor,** soldiers are awarded service ribbons and medals. Some, like the Silver Star, are for bravery. The Purple Heart medal means the wearer was wounded in action.

The highest award is the Medal of Honor, for acts of bravery over and above the call of duty.

"Are soldiers ever scared?" asked Jake.

"Of course," said Dad. "I think every soldier is scared at one time or another. I was scared plenty of times when I was a soldier. We all were."

"Then how can you be brave? I don't get it!"

"Jake, just because you may feel scared, it doesn't mean you can't be brave."

Jake nodded. Then some gold and silver badges caught his eye.

"Can I have one of those, too?" he asked.

"Sure. Those are marksmanship badges for being a good shot," said Dad.

Small arms and light weapons (SALW) are the tools of the trade for soldiers. Prehistoric humans first used sticks and sharpened stones to fight and hunt. Over time, more advanced weapons such as knives, spears, and bows and arrows were developed. Today's soldier uses modern, high-tech weapons such as assault rifles, grenade launchers, and anti-tank and aircraft guns.

Jake and Dad continued through the store. Jake's eyes widened when he spotted a huge vest.

"That's body armor. It protects the soldiers," said Dad.

As weapons developed, armies needed to devise new ways to protect their soldiers. Shields protected against clubs and arrows. **Suits of armor** offered some protection against swords and spears. However, these methods were not as effective against weapons that used gunpowder, such as guns, grenades, and cannons. Suits of armor were also very heavy and cumbersome.

Today's **body armor and helmets** are made of strong but lightweight composite material, which helps to protect soldiers against the dangers of modern warfare.

Jake picked up a helmet with a Captain's insignia and tried it on for size. "Can I have this?"

"Wouldn't you rather have a soldier's cap?"

"But this helmet is so awesome!" said Jake.

"Ok, Captain, it's yours," said Dad.

Then Jake came to something he thought was really cool.

"Look at this!" he exclaimed, holding up a gas mask.

"I don't know," said Dad.

"Please, please, please," said Jake. "It can be my birthday present."

"You just had your birthday," said Dad.

"Then it can count for next year!"

Dad scratched his head, thoughtfully. "It is pretty cool. Ok," he agreed.

Then Jake found a pair of binoculars. *This place has so much awesome stuff.* "Look at these!" he said. "Can I have these, too? I love these binoculars."

Dad said, "You don't need everything you see. You can pick either the binoculars or the mask, but not both."

Jake thought about it and said, "I'll take the gas mask." *I really want the binoculars, too,* he thought. *But, I can't believe I'm getting the gas mask!*

The gas mask protects the wearer's face and eyes from airborne pollutants and chemical or biological hazards.

Sometimes armies use poison gas against an enemy. Some gases are designed to burn the eyes while others can choke you. To block the gas, the masks fit tight on the face. Most have an air filter. One of the most common filters is made of charcoal. Other gas masks have hoses that attach to air tanks to help a soldier breathe safely.

As Dad and Jake continued through the store, they came up to tons of boots. Jake asked, "Can I get Army boots? Mom said I needed new shoes anyway."

"You always seem to need new shoes," said Dad. "I guess that means you're growing. Let's see if they have your size."

Boots are basic to soldiers, and Basic Training for soldiers is called **Boot Camp.**

Boot Camp is an eight-week period when men and women learn to be soldiers. Along with tough physical training, new recruits study teamwork, military tactics, survival skills, and marksmanship in order to become combat-ready troops.

Boot Camp training is led by **Drill Sergeants.** They are like very strict school teachers. Their job is to make a soldier out of you.

"Look, they have kids' boots, too," said Dad.

"Great," said Jake, and he picked out a pair of black boots. "I feel a lot taller in them," he said.

"Soldiers do stand a lot taller," said Dad, smiling.

After everything was paid for, Jake and his dad headed home. Jake spent the rest of Saturday and most of Sunday trying on his uniform and helping his mom sew on the patches and place the ribbons.

When Monday morning finally arrived, Jake got dressed up in his new Army uniform, complete with ribbons, patches, medals, pins, boots, and gas mask.

"How do I look?" Jake asked.

"You look rough and ready, just like a soldier," said Dad.

"I am ready!" Jake said.

"But do you think the class might hear you more clearly if you're not wearing the gas mask? Maybe just carry it."

"Dad, you're going to be very proud of me when
I get an 'A,'" said Jake, taking off the mask. "Will
you be even more proud if I'm a real U.S. Army
soldier when I grow up?"

"I'm already proud of you, son. I will be no matter
what you do when you grow up," said Dad.

Jake knew that already, but he liked to hear it
anyway.

At school, Jake waited for his turn to give his presentation. He was nervous and excited at the same time.

His classmates were wearing costumes and carrying posters and bags. Hannah was sitting at her desk with a poster and her backpack.

"Hannah, what did you pick?" asked Jake.

"You'll find out," said Hannah. "Cool uniform, Jake."

Jake grinned. "Thanks! We got it at the Army surplus store."

"The one on 17th Street?" asked Hannah.

"Yeah," said Jake. He was surprised that Hannah knew about the store.

When Jake's turn finally came, he walked to the front of the class.

On the way, his friend Tommy said, "Nice gas mask!"

Then Jake began, "Today I am going to talk about why I want to be a U.S. Army soldier when I grow up."

Jake told his class about all he had learned at the Army surplus store, from the Infantry, to the weapons, to the suits of armor.

"But most of all," said Jake, "I want to talk about the soldiers and how brave they are.

"The soldiers of the United States Army protect us and our way of life. They keep us safe from bad guys who want to tell us what to do. Soldiers are brave. They have to be away from their families, and sometimes they get into danger. We should be very proud of our soldiers. They are real-life heroes!"

The teacher said, "Very well done, Jake. Thank you. I am sure everyone in class enjoyed your presentation."

When Jake sat down, Hannah even gave him a "high five." She had never done that before.

When it was Hannah's turn to give her presentation, she stood up, holding her poster and backpack.

What does she have in the backpack? Jake wondered.

The whole class watched as Hannah walked to the front of the room. She reached into her backpack and pulled out something that looked very familiar.

The Army binoculars!

Hannah put the binoculars around her neck and held up her poster. She smiled at Jake. The poster had pictures of tanks, helicopters, and Army patches. On the very bottom in neat handwritten letters it read, "Go Army."

So that's why Hannah knows all about the Army surplus store! thought Jake.

Jake listened to Hannah talk all about the Army. Hannah spoke about training and about how both men and women serve in the Army. She talked about how soldiers help rescue people in trouble. He thought that her project was really good and that her poster was really cool.

But mostly he thought, *I wonder if she'll let me borrow those binoculars!*

Glossary

Army - A large military force trained for combat on land.

Artillery - Large-caliber weapons, such as cannons, howitzers, and missile launchers, that are operated by crews, and the name of the branch of the Army that specializes in the use of such weapons.

BCT - Basic Combat Training, or Basic Training. The first eight weeks of training for new recruits, also known as Boot Camp.

BDU - Battle dress uniform. The standard uniform for combat situations.

Cavalry - Historically refers to warriors who fought mounted on horseback. Cavalry today refers to any Army component moving in motor vehicles or helicopters and assigned to combat missions that require great mobility.

Class A Uniform - Army dress uniform sometimes worn for office-type work.

CO - Commanding Officer. The officer in charge of the military unit, or base.

Commissioned Officers - Leaders of the Army.

Fatigues - Old term to describe the battle and work uniform.

GI - Government Issue. A term first used to describe government equipment and often used to describe soldiers.

Infantry - The branch of an army made up of units trained to fight on foot.

Marksmanship - Skill at firing at a target.

MLRS - Multiple Launch Rocket System.

MP - Military Police.

NCO - Non-Commissioned Officer. An enlisted person with command responsibility over soldiers of lesser rank.

PT - Physical training. Used in the plural (PTs), it refers to the PT uniform.

PX - Post Exchange. A multipurpose store on an Army base which usually includes a barber shop and a convenience store.

Rank - The named title of a soldier with a particular grade and responsibility, such as Private, Specialist, Staff Sergeant, Captain, etc.

Recruit - A new soldier in training, especially Basic Training.

Tank - A tracked, armored fighting vehicle for frontline combat generally armed with a high-power cannon and a turret with secondary machine guns.

CPSIA information can be obtained
at www.ICGtesting.com
Printed in the USA
LVHW070354060820
662527LV00017B/1774